TITLE IX ROCKS!
PLAY LIKE A GIRL™

TRACK AND FIELD

GIRLS ROCKING IT

MYRNA CARROLL and CLAUDIA B. MANLEY

rosen publishing's
rosen central®
New York

Published in 2016 by The Rosen Publishing Group, Inc.
29 East 21st Street, New York, NY 10010

First Edition

Library of Congress CataloginginPublication Data

Carroll, Myrna.
 Track and field : girls rocking it / Myrna Carroll and Claudia B. Manley.—First Edition.
      pages cm. — ((Title IX Rocks! Play Like a Girl))
 Includes index.
 ISBN 978-1-5081-7043-3 (Library bound)
 1. Track and field for women—Juvenile literature. I. Manley, Claudia B. II. Title.
 GV1060.8.C37 2015
 796.42082–dc23

                                                      2015016583

Manufactured in China

CONTENTS

N o person in the United States shall, on the basis of sex, be excluded from participation in, be denied the benefits of, or be subjected to discrimination under any education program or activity receiving federal financial assistance." This is the clause of the Education Amendments of 1972, referred to as Title IX. It was signed into law by President Richard Nixon on June 23 of that year and had its greatest impact on collegiate athletics, ensuring that the ratio of female to male athletes matched that of the student body. Since then, there have been several attempts to amend the law, as well as lawsuits against schools that have refused to comply with it.

Opponents to the law continued to challenge it. They achieved a short-lived victory in 1984 in the suit *Grove City v. Bell* in which the judge ruled that Title IX affected only programs that received federal assistance directly. The law was overturned four years later when the Civil Rights Restoration Act overrode *Grove City v. Bell.* More than thirty-five years after the law was signed, challenges continue to be lobbied. As recently as in 2009, the U.S. Supreme Court ruled in favor of parents in *Fitzgerald v. Barnstable School Committee,* stating that the parents could sue for sex discrimination in schools under Title IX and the Equal Protection Clause of the Constitution. Before Title IX, female track and field athletes were regularly discriminated

Since Title IX was enacted into law by President Nixon, it has been challenged several times in the courts. In 2006, students from James Madison University protest cuts to some of their athletic teams.

against in national and international games, and had few governing bodies supervising their sport.

Although there is no record of the early days of track and field, it is considered to be one of the oldest sports. Pole vaulting is believed to have debuted at the Tailteann Games in Ireland in 1829 BCE. A similar event to the shot put was also said to have occurred during the siege of Troy in 1000 BCE during a rock-throwing contest. Organized athletic contests were often held in conjunction with religious festivals such as the Olympic Games. The first official marathon was run at the Olympic Games in 776 BCE, however women were forbidden at the games, even as spectators. One woman named Kallipateira dressed as a trainer to see her son compete, and thereafter, all athletes and trainers were forced to strip before entering the stadium to ensure no woman ever attended again.

However, a series of races held in honor of the Greek goddess Hera afforded unmarried women an opportunity to show their track and field prowess. The Sixteen Women, a council of representatives of each city of the ancient state of Elis hosted the competition every four years. The footraces pitted women of the same age against each other, with the youngest racers going first. The women used the same stadium as the Olympic Games, and the races and participants were well respected, but they did not have the same prestige as the Olympic Games. Not much has changed in that regard. Male track and field athletes regularly get more endorsement deals than their female counterparts.

Modern track and field was developed in England as early as 1154 CE, with everyone, even royalty participating. King Henry VIII was known as a very good hammer thrower. The sport spread in the 1800s to North America and became truly international when the Olympic Games were revived in 1896. Female athletes, however, did not have the same opportunities to compete. International track and field events were governed by the International Amateur Athletic Federation (IAAF), which was founded in 1912 by representatives from sixteen countries, but it did not include events for women. In 1921, representatives from six countries formed an athletic federation for women that merged with the IAAF twenty-four years after it was founded, and finally brought women's events under their jurisdiction. The discrimination against female athletes remained prevalent internationally until the United States Congress passed the Education Amendments, including Title IX in 1972. The United States has led the way in women's track and field because of Title IX, despite the fact that the law continues to be challenged to this day.

CHAPTER ONE

WHAT IS TRACK AND FIELD?

M ost people probably think of running when they think of track and field, but there is so much more to this sport than just tests of speed. Track and field sports involve running, racewalking, jumping, and throwing, and sometimes, some combination of these. Track events are distance-based speed tests. Women's events are usually broken into the following distances: 100, 200, 400, 800, 1,500, 5,000, and 10,000 meters. Track also includes jumping hurdles with distances of 100 and 400 meters, and relay events at distances of 400 and 1,500 meters. Olympic racewalking covers a distance of 20 kilometers, but there are some shorter distance events. Field events include the jumping competitions high jump, long jump, and pole vault, as well as throwing competitions such as shot put, discus, hammer, and javelin. Track and field athletes can also participate in the heptathlon, a seven-event

Women compete in a 55-meter dash in Landover, Maryland. The winner (*center*) was Ajai Brooks of Washington, D.C.

competition combining 100-meter hurdles, high jump, shot put, 200-meter dash, long jump, javelin throw, and an 800-meter run.

WHAT YOU NEED FOR TRACK AND FIELD

All track and field events require shoes that grip the track or launch surface, and protect the foot while still being lightweight. You should select shoes that fit well and perform under your event's conditions. Other equipment you might invest in could be a javelin, a vaulting

pole, or any of the other throwing implements. The cost of these items can range anywhere from $30 up to $250 or more.

Many schools have track and field teams; however, they may not field a team that competes in all events. If you can't find a team at your school, check with USA Track and Field or Athletics Canada to see if there's a recreational youth team you could join.

An official outdoor track is a 400-meter (440 yards) oval. The actual track surface can be dirt, clay, or crushed brick. All major competition tracks have surfaces made of synthetic materials. These provide better and more consistent footing in all weather conditions. Jumpers and javelin throwers also compete on a synthetic

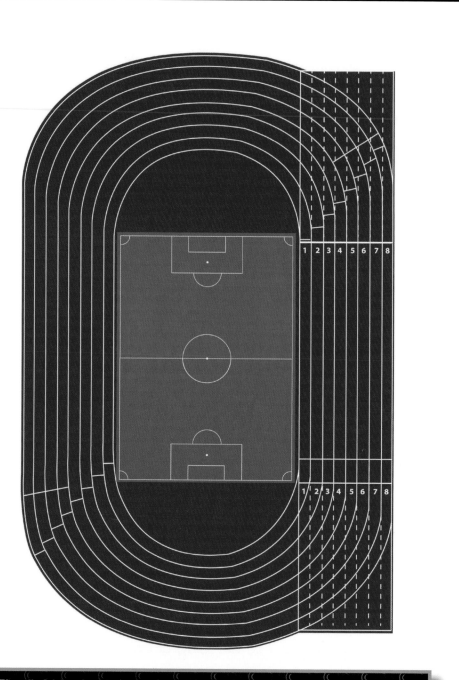

The field is multi-purpose. Staggered starting lines can be seen at the top right and lower left. The open area in the center is used for shot put, high jump, and other sports.

surface, while athletes in the shot put, discus, and hammer throws use concrete circles. Indoor tracks range in size from 150 to 200 meters (160–220 yards) and have a synthetic surface over wood. Cross-country events use any available terrain, including roads, parks, and golf courses.

TRACK EVENTS

If you're quick and can use all of your energy in a relatively short burst, then sprinting may be your skill. A sprint is a race up to 400 meters. A sprinter performs at top speed from start to finish. All runners must have their hands and feet on the track at the start. Starting blocks, which are rigid supports where runners place their rear foot, give runners something to push off to get a quick start. They are required for races up to and including the 400-meter run. Runners are staggered; that means that they start at different points on the track to equalize the distance to the finish. The track is an oval, so the outside lane is longer. A sprinter in the outside lane, which is the lane farthest from the center, will start slightly farther up the track. The staggered starting line accommodates the track's curve. Runners must stay in their lanes, except in races longer than one lap. The runner whose torso crosses the finish line first, wins.

Mid-distance runs (those between 800 and 2,000 meters) require both the quickness of a sprinter and the endurance of the long-distance runner. These events also require a good understanding of race tactics such as pacing, which allows you to save just enough energy to sprint to the finish.

If you have the power to run for a long time, then the long dis-tance runs—races longer than 3,000 meters—could be your events. These require less speed but more pacing and endurance. They are rarely finished with the kind of sprint you see in mid-distance runs.

Gateshead International Stadium

This young hurdler competes in a junior championship in Gateshead, England.

The marathon is the longest race of a track meet and is 42,186 meters, or 26 miles and 385 yards (commonly referred to as 26.2 miles). It was one of the main events of the first Olympics and is named for the legendary run of a Greek soldier in 490 BCE, who ran from the city of Marathon to Athens to bring news of a Greek victory over the Persians. It was also a key event when the modern Olympics were revived in Paris in 1896.

Hurdling combines sprinting speed with the agility to jump over a series of obstacles called hurdles. The 100-meter high hurdles consist of ten hurdles that are forty-two inches high and spaced ten yards apart. The 400-meter intermediate hurdles also have ten hurdles, but they are only thirty-six inches high and spaced 38.29 yards (35 meters) apart. A runner may accidentally knock down hurdles during the race but will be disqualified if she uses her hand to knock them over. You don't want to knock them down as that breaks your stride. The steeplechase combines hurdling with long distance running. Over a 3,000-meter course, athletes must clear seven water jumps and twenty-eight hurdles. Because of its unique nature, athletes who run the steeplechase often only participate in this one event.

FANNY BLANKERS-KOEN

Fanny Blankers-Koen was the first woman to win four gold medals at one Olympic Games, which she did at age thirty and after having had two children. Blankers-Koen was battling the perception that women athletes were not feminine—a fact the media said was disproved by her status as a married mother of two—and the perception that she was too old to race. Ultimately, neither her age nor her femininity proved to have any influence at all on her ability. Blankers-Koen competed in twelve competitions in the 1948 Olympics. She won gold medals in the 100-meter race, the 80-meter hurdle, the 200-meter race, and the 4x100-meter relay. She did not compete in the long jump and high jump, though she may have won gold in these two if she had. Her world record in both of these was not broken at that year's Olympics.

Blankers-Koen is pictured in 1950, two years after her record Olympic Games. She performed in the high jump and broke the record in the 200-meter race.

If you have speed, coordination, timing, and a good sense of teamwork, the relay event might be for you. The two standard relay events are the 100- and the 400-meter relays. Relays have four runners per team and divide the running so that each girl runs 25 percent of the race. Passing the baton to your teammate requires coordination and timing on both the passer's and the receiver's part. A smooth and well-timed transition often makes the difference between a win and a loss. The 200-, 800-, and 1,500-meter relays aren't run as regularly.

Race walking is not always a part of a track meet although it is included in the Olympic Games as well as other multinational events. In race walking, if both feet leave the ground at the same time, the walker is disqualified for running. Olympic distances are over 20,000 and 50,000 meters, but individual meets may set other distances.

FIELD EVENTS

Field events fall into two categories: jumping and throwing. The four jumping events are the high jump, pole vault, long jump, and triple jump. The throwing events are the shot put, discus throw, hammer throw, and javelin throw. As of the 2000 Olympics in Sydney, women could compete in all field events.

The object of the high jump is to clear a thin rail supported by two stands. The jumper must leave the ground from one foot, not spring off from both feet. She can start at any height above the minimum set by the judges. As long as she doesn't miss three jumps in a row, she stays in the competition.

Jump techniques include the scissors, the western roll, and the belly flop. The most universally used technique is the Fosbury flop, named after 1968 United States Olympic champion Dick Fosbury: The jumper approaches the bar almost straight on, twists on takeoff, and goes over the bar headfirst, with her back to the bar. Stefka Kostadinova of Bulgaria was the record holder as of 2015 with a jump of 2.09 meters. She has also held on to her record for the longest period since 1987.

The 2000 Sydney Olympics saw the debut of the pole-vault competition for women. Stacy Dragila of the United States was the first woman to win a gold medal in the event. As in the high jump, a pole-vaulter has three tries at each height to clear the bar. The vaulter races down a runway carrying a fiberglass pole. As she plants the end of the pole in a box sunken slightly below the ground, she pulls herself up and almost over the pole (like a handstand). As she nears the bar, she twists and arches so that her feet go over first and she is facing downward. Pole jumpers may compete outdoors or indoors. In 2009, Yelena Isinbayeva of Russia achieved the women's outdoor world record of 5.06 meters, while Jennifer Suhr of the United States achieved the indoor record of 5.02 meters in 2013.

Speed is the most important element in the long jump. The runner approaches the takeoff board at top speed, plants one foot on it and leaps across the sandpit, often using a technique that looks as if she's running in the air. The jumper must make sure that no part of her leading foot extends beyond the takeoff board or the jump will be disallowed.

The triple jump was once known as the hop, step, and jump, referring to the three distinct segments of the event. Running toward the takeoff board, the competitor bounds off. She lands on the same foot she took off on and springs off of it. In the next motion she steps landing on the opposite foot and finally jumps into the sand pit.

In the shot put, the athlete "puts" a four kilogram (eight pounds thirteen ounces) metal shot that is about ten centimeters in diameter. The "put" is not traditional throwing; it's more like shoving from the shoulder. The arm cannot extend behind the shoulder. The putter (as the athlete is called) gets the momentum up by twisting rapidly inside the two-meter (seven-foot) shot put ring. Shot putters are generally among the largest and strongest of the track and field athletes because of the strength that's required.

The discus throw is considered a classic event because of historical references in literature and art. Competitors launch a one-kilogram plate-like disc from within a two-meter (eight feet two inches) circle after completing one and a half turns.

In the hammer throw, you don't really pitch a hammer. You throw a metal ball about 127 millimeters (5 inches) in diameter attached by a wire to a handle. The whole thing weighs around 7.26 kilograms (16 pounds). Holding just the handle, the thrower whips up centrifugal force by spinning around three or four times and then lets it fly.

An athlete competes in a javelin throw event.

The launching area is just a little smaller than the discus throw area. Lamila Skolimowska of Poland won the first women's gold medal when the sport was debuted at the 2000 Sydney Olympics.

In the javelin throw, an athlete hurls a spear known as a javelin with all her strength. The women's javelin weighs at least 600 grams (1.3 pounds) and is at least 220 centimeters (7.2 feet) long. This is the only throwing event that does not use a launching circle. The javelin does not have to stick into the ground to be valid, but does have to land with its point first.

The seven-event heptathlon takes place over two days with participants scored on their performance in each event. The heptathlon replaced the women's pentathlon in the Olympic Games after 1981, which featured five events. On the first day of the heptathlon, the athletes compete in the 100-meter hurdles, the high jump, shot put, and a 200-meter sprint. The second day features the long jump, as well as javelin throw, and an 800-meter run. The most notable heptathlete is American Jackie Joyner-Kersee, a two-time Olympic gold medalist.

Kersee, born on March 3, 1962, competed in women's heptathlons as well as the long jump. Her career highlights included winning three gold, one silver, and two bronze medals in the Olympics over the course of four different Olympic Games. Sports Illustrated for Women magazine named her the Greatest Female Athlete of the twentieth century.

CHAPTER TWO

TRAINING FOR TRACK AND FIELD

Because there are many elements to the events in track and field, it is important for athletes to have good overall conditioning. A good training program will include stretching, strength and endurance training, improving aerobic ability, and cardiovascular endurance. Athletes also need to concentrate on running form and technique, including best practices for different types of starts such as starting from a standing position, or starting crouched at the starting block. Managing pacing and making a race plan—as well as focusing on the mechanics of running, takeoff, approach, grip stance, baton exchanges, and landing—are also important aspects of full training in track and field. A good program will cover all of these and more.

Your heart's ability to deliver blood to your muscles over an extended period of time is measured by your cardiovascular

Because track and field events require many different skills, athletes usually cross-train doing several different strength, endurance, and stretching exercises.

endurance. Of course, track events require a strong heart whether you're a sprinter or a marathon runner, but many of the field events have running starts as well. Although the runways might be relatively short, think about how often you may have to run them if you successfully advance in a meet. It would be pretty disappointing if you didn't have the cardiovascular endurance necessary to make it to the runway for the deciding jump!

Any exercise that raises your heart rate and keeps it raised for at least twenty minutes benefits your cardiovascular system. You want to get that kind of workout at least three times a week. If you have track and field practice that often, you're probably set. Biking or skating are also good ways to condition your heart.

STRENGTH AND ENDURANCE TRAINING

Strength and endurance are key factors in any training program for a track and field athlete. Strength training (also called weight training) is particularly very important. Basic strength training will not only increase your strength but also give you a leaner body mass. Training with weights is also important for women because it helps strengthen bones. Women suffer from a higher rate of osteoporosis (bone density loss) than men, which can result in increased injuries from bone breaks.

Strength training should be done at least three times a week. Pay attention to your posture and breathing, and work your muscles smoothly. You can do most of the following exercises without going to a gym if you have free weights or dumbbells. Start with weights that require a bit of effort to lift but aren't so heavy that you can only do one set of repetitions. It's better to start lighter and increase weight than to strain your muscles trying too much too soon. Each exercise can be done in sets of fifteen for two or three repetitions. This is the endurance part of the training. As soon as a weight feels light, switch to a slightly heavier one.

Among the best exercises for strength and endurance training are crunches, pushups, toe and leg raises, squats, lunges, and high-knee skipping. Most of these can be done with or without the use of weights for resistance.

WORKING SPECIFIC BODY PARTS

Different exercises work on specific muscle groups to ensure strength and flexibility. Depending on an athlete's physical condition and specific needs, a trainer may choose to focus more on one area than others. The following are good basics for a full-body

Before starting any exercise, it is always a good idea to stretch and warm up your muscles. Failing to do so can result in injuries.

workout concentrating on one area at a time starting from the legs and moving up.

Quadriceps, Hamstrings, and Hips

A good exercise for the big muscles in your thighs is the lunge. Stand with feet parallel but slightly apart, a weight in each hand. Take a big step forward with your right foot without stretching or losing your balance. Slowly lower your left knee to the floor. Rise and return to the starting position. Switch legs and repeat. Another good exercise is squats. With your legs apart, bend at the knee. Make sure not to bend more than 90 degrees. Rise to standing.

Calves

To strengthen your calves, begin in a standing position with a weight in each hand. Slowly raise your heels untill you are balanced on your toes. Hold for ten seconds. Lower yourself back to the starting position.

Shoulders

To do the shoulder shrug, start as before, with a weight in each hand. Raise your shoulders to your ears as though you were shrugging. Hold for ten seconds and release slowly.

Arms

The bench press is good for your arms and pectoral muscles. Lie on your back on the bench with your knees bent and a weight in each hand. Your arms should be bent with your hand resting at your shoulders. With a slow, smooth motion, push the weight away from you so that your arms are extended straight above your shoulders. Slowly lower them back down.

The bicep curl can be performed seated or standing. Hold a dumbbell in each hand with your palms facing outwards, back straight, and feet on the floor. Slowly curl the weight toward your shoulders by bending at the elbows. Lower the weight slowly to the starting position. Repeat with the opposite arm.

For the tricep kickback hold a dumbbell in your right hand with the palm facing inward. Bending at the waist until your upper body is almost parallel with the floor, place your left hand on a bench or on your upper thigh for support. Bend your knees slightly and keep your stomach muscles tight.

Raise your right elbow and upper arm to the back, keeping your elbow tight to your body. Press the dumbbell backward, straightening your elbow until your entire arm is parallel to the floor. Hold briefly, then lower the weight. Perform one complete set, and then repeat with the opposite arm.

STRETCHING

Stretching helps make your muscles more elastic and increases your flexibility. Never stretch cold muscles. Warm them up with a light jog, by jumping rope, or by giving them a massage. A shower is another way to warm the muscles.

Here are a few exercises you can try. Make sure that you stretch the muscles and don't bounce. Breathe deeply and stretch until you feel a mild pull but no pain. Hold each stretch for fifteen to twenty seconds, then rest for about ten. Repeat three times.

Calf Muscles

Stand about two feet away from a wall, a tree, or any other sturdy structure. Step back about a foot with your right foot. Bend your left knee and lean toward the wall, keeping your back straight and your heels flat on the ground. Your right leg should be straight and you should feel a stretch in the right calf. You can move your left foot forward a bit to get more of a stretch if you need to. Return to the starting position and repeat with the opposite leg.

Hamstring

Lie on your back and bring your left knee to your chest. Gently hold the back of your thigh with both hands and press your thigh into them. Keep the thigh muscle contracted and slowly extend your left foot to the ceiling until your leg is straight. Point your heel toward the ceiling. Keep the right leg extended, with the right thigh pressing down and toes pointing up. Switch legs and repeat.

Quadriceps

Face forward, bend your right knee, and grab your right ankle with your right hand. Bring your heel to your butt with your right knee pointing at the floor. You should feel a mild stretch along the front of your right leg. Hold this for twenty seconds and then switch legs.

If you don't have very good balance, get a partner to help. Stand face to face and balance each other by putting your left hand (when you're stretching your right leg) on your partner's right shoulder.

Inner Thigh/Groin

Sit on the floor, soles of your feet together, your heels at a comfortable distance from your groin. Holding your feet, place your elbows on your legs and bend forward slowly from your hips. Try not to round your lower back. You should feel a stretch in your groin area. As your muscles relax and this stretch gets easier, increase pressure on your legs with your elbows.

Shoulders

Raise your right arm. Bend it at the elbow so that your right hand is behind your head and your right elbow is pointing upwards. With your left hand gently pull your right elbow behind your head and toward the left. Let your right hand slide down your back. Keep your shoulders down and relaxed. Hold the stretch, then switch arms.

Using simple equipment such as this stretch band adds resistance to your workout, which is a good way to do conditioning without a lot of stress to your muscles.

USING OTHER SPORTS FOR TRAINING

Many athletes do other types of sports as part of their training. This is called cross-training. It gives you the opportunity to try some-thing new. You will be amazed at how different an activity can be when you're not focused on competing.

Ride your bike leisurely, warming up for a few minutes. Then stand up and pedal as fast as you can for thirty seconds. Sit down and pedal slowly to recover and then try it again, maybe for forty-five seconds this time. Build up to one minute of this high-powered pedaling and then taper back down to thirty seconds. Cool down with a leisurely ride.

Yoga is an excellent cross-training option. Besides giving you increased flexibility, it also strengthens muscles and encourages you to focus on the moment. This frees your mind from obsessing about all those details that usually race through it. Walking and hik-ing are also good ways to cross-train.

TYPICAL TRACK AND FIELD INJURIES

Because track and field encompasses so many events, there are many opportunities for injury. We'll focus on some of the most com-mon ones.

Stress fractures are small breaks in the bone that come from repeated stress and are most common in the leg bones (tibia, meta-tarsals, and fibula). Fractures in the foot bones are most common among sprinters and hurdlers. A sudden increase in the intensity of training (increasing how many miles you run), introducing a new activity (such as hill training), a change of environment (switching from paths in the park to streets), and bad equipment (worn-out running shoes) all can contribute to stress fractures. Women are more susceptible to this type of injury if they have low bone density (osteoporosis), menstrual irregularities, or poor diets.

Basic treatment requires rest from the activity that caused the injury for about four to eight weeks. You can keep up your conditioning by cycling or weight training. It's important for you and your doctor to figure out what caused the fracture in the first place so that you don't repeat the same mistake.

When you can walk normally and there's no tenderness in the area of the fracture, you can begin a gradual return to your sport. If you had to stop running, for instance, you might start out with long walks, then jogging, and then return to your normal running pace.

Stress fractures of the foot generally require a non-weight-bearing cast for at least six weeks. After that an additional six-week rehabilitation program follows to strengthen the area and give a gradual return to the sport.

ACL (anterior cruciate ligament, which is a part of your knee) injuries, when the ligament tears, are particularly high for women involved in jumping sports. One cause is landing with a straight leg (with your knee locked). Learning to flex your knee when landing will help prevent this injury. Depending upon the severity of the tear, treatment can range from rest and immobilization to an operation to repair the tear. Recuperation time can last from five or six weeks to months if you've had surgery.

The shoulder joint sustains injury in sports involving over hand actions such as throwing. The most common is an irritation of the rotator cuff and the surrounding soft tissue. Some of the symptoms of shoulder injury are a numbing pain throughout the arm, unusual sounds (such as cracking or popping) when you rotate your shoulder, pain when doing something simple such as throwing a ball, and an inability to raise your arm above 90 degrees. One theory why shoulder injuries are more common in female athletes is that

COMPETING WITH AN INJURY

It is not unheard of for athletes to compete despite injuries, but it is inadvisable. Performing on an injured body part can cause irreparable damage and could end an athlete's career. Athletes are advised to follow doctor's orders following an injury to make sure that they heal properly, but sometimes a meet is coming up, and an athlete wants to perform. They may ignore the better advice to take the time they

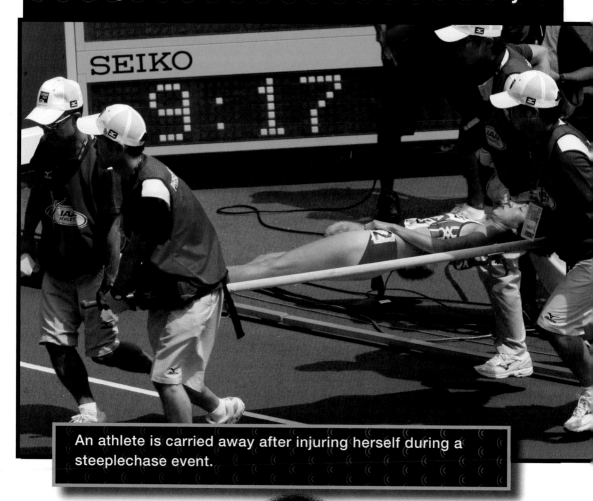

An athlete is carried away after injuring herself during a steeplechase event.

need to heal. Athletes may think of stories such as that of Alice Coachman, who made history as the first black woman to win an Olympic medal and win a major endorsement deal. Coachman attended the 1948 Olympics in London and broke the world record high jump at 5 feet 6⅛ inches, despite working through a back injury. But more often than not, athletes do not have this kind of success despite an injury. There will always be other meets and other opportunities to perform.

they are not encouraged to strengthen their upper bodies, and thus, their shoulder muscles are not prepared to take physical stress.

Treatment depends on the severity of the injury. You might be given a painkiller or anti-inflammatory (something that reduces muscle swelling) drug, or even a shot of cortisone (a prescription anti-inflammatory drug). Shoulder injuries require a lot of rest, which can be anywhere from eight weeks up. You should also get a rehabilitation program that involves progressive strengthening of the area to help you regain full use and movement in your shoulder.

Hamstring (the muscle on the back of your thigh) injuries are often seen in track and field athletes because many of the events require quick bursts of speed. Not warming up properly, being tired, and having poor flexibility all contribute to these injuries. Luckily, the majority can be treated through RICE—rest, ice, compression, and elevation. Putting an elastic wrap around the area can help reduce swelling, and a painkiller such as acetaminophen (e.g., Tylenol) should alleviate any discomfort. If you're still in pain, see your doctor. Unfortunately, it takes a while to recover from any hamstring injury and the recurrence is high.

Runners often encounter sharp pains along the front or inside of the lower leg. These are called shin splints and are the result of muscle and tendon weakness caused by any number of factors, including increasing mileage too quickly, running on hard surfaces, or downhill running. Shin splints can be treated with rest, ice, and anti-inflammatory medications such as Advil. Prevention comes through strengthening the muscles of the lower leg and avoiding overtraining.

CHAPTER THREE

BEYOND THE PHYSICAL

As a teen, you encounter a lot of pressure. Maybe your parents want you to succeed in track and field, maybe your classmates don't think you have what it takes, or maybe you doubt yourself. The desire to prove yourself can be a strong force in overtraining. Between school teams, personal trainers, and summer sports camps, you can find yourself training year-round.

When you overtrain, your body has no time to recover. You start to fatigue (wear down) muscles and leave yourself open to injury. Frustrated, you ignore your body's warning signs: missed periods, chronic pain, and even decreased performance. Overtraining can be as detrimental as an injury. The best way to recuperate is to rest. You don't have to be totally inactive, but take a break from track and field and try something different and less stressful, such as swimming or yoga. Gradually come back to your training, but increase your intensity slowly or you can risk re-injury.

Many injuries can be avoided through proper training and technique. You don't want to have to sit out a meet just because you didn't warm up properly when you went for a training run the other day, nor do you want to risk a shoulder injury because you're afraid lifting weights will make you big or bulky.

Listen to your body. Take it easy if you've had a tough workout and are tired. It doesn't make you a better athlete if you play through pain because in the end you and your team will suffer even more from your future absence at the meet after an injury.

MENTAL TRAINING

Track and field isn't just about the physical. In order to excel, you need to work on your mental game as well. Perhaps the most important aspect of this is attitude. The difference between being a negative person and having a positive attitude can be the difference between performing poorly and performing well.

Sometimes it's hard not to beat yourself up over your performance and it feels impossible to be positive. In these times, having a phrase that gives you confidence can be a great help. Try saying something like, "If I don't give up, then I've already succeeded." Or if you're becoming tired, just tell yourself, "I'm almost there, I can do it." (Just remember that fatigue may also mean you need a break.)

Focus is also important. If you have goals for yourself, such as finishing a race in a certain time or jumping a specific height, focusing on these will help you achieve them, keeping you motivated.

If you're having difficulty with your event, it often helps to think about it—to visualize it. Professional athletes use visualization techniques to help them perform better. For example, if you're nervous

Some of the preparation for an event happens in your head. You need to be mentally prepared to compete and do well.

about knocking over the hurdles, imagine your perfect race. What would it look like? One of the benefits of visualization is that you can slow down, repeat, or even stop the action in your head. You can see yourself at the beginning of the race, your powerful start, your approach to the hurdle, and your follow-through. Visualization helps you to learn the event mentally, which makes it easier to put it into practice physically.

PROPER NUTRITION

There's nothing worse than "bonking" (running out of energy) at a critical moment because you decided that one cheese danish would last you all day. To participate in a track and field meet, which might keep you active for most of the day, you need to provide the proper fuel for your body.

A general rule for a young athlete is to get around 60 percent of your diet from carbohydrates. If you're a long-distance runner, you might increase that to 75 percent. "Carbs" are an athlete's main source of fuel. The body changes carbs into glucose, a form of sugar, and stores it in your muscles as glycogen. As you exercise, glycogen changes into energy. Depending on your training or event needs, you may need to increase your carbohydrate intake up to three or four days before, and you may need to adjust your carbohydrate intake even hours before an event depending on what your body needs. Scheduling your eating around your meet is a good strategy. Figure out what works best for your body. Do you do well eating an English muffin with peanut butter an hour before your event, or is it better to have an egg and some toast three hours before? Don't experiment on the day of a meet! Most athletes like to eat something one to four hours before their event. It's also good to eat something right after an event, since your muscles need to take in more fuel at that time.

Just remember that what works for another athlete may not work for you. You will have to see how your body reacts to food to determine what it needs to perform at its peak.

Athletes generally require more protein than the average individual because of the muscle built during training. Protein also provides long-term energy, vitamins, and minerals. It also helps to repair tissue. Protein comes from animal sources such as meat, cheese, and fish, and non-animal sources, such as tofu and other soy products.

Fats are necessary in everyone's diet but they shouldn't contribute more than 30 percent of your daily calories. Many athletes choose a low-fat diet,

A healthy breakfast of fruit and grains will give you what you need on regular training days. On meet days, you may need to change your intake slightly.

which keeps their intake to between 10 and 15 percent. However, remember that your body is still developing. Check with your doctor before changing your diet.

Calcium is very important for young women, particularly since they don't often get enough of it from their regular diet. Calcium helps prevent osteoporosis, which can affect the young just as easily as the old. Calcium supplements ensure that you get the

It's important to listen to your body to make sure that you get enough water, and rest between events so that you do not put undue strain on your body.

recommended dosage of between 1,200 and 1,500 milligrams a day.

Make sure you drink lots of water before, during, and after your competition. Dehydration can be a serious issue and water helps keep your system functioning smoothly. Some endurance athletes, like long-distance runners, will often have a sports drink during their race as well. But remember that eating sugary or starchy foods within thirty minutes of an event or the beginning an exercise routine can speed up dehydration and undermine all of your hard work.

Unfortunately, images in magazines and on television reinforce the ideal of a thin young woman. Track and field uniforms can be revealing, making some girls feel self-conscious. An unhealthy preoccupation with weight can result in the female athlete triad—a combination of eating disorders (such as bulimia or anorexia), low bone density, and missed periods. Sometimes athletes become obsessed with controlling their weight because they can't control the outcome of their games. Being healthy and strong is one of the most important things for an athlete. Eating disorders destroy your health because your body is not getting proper nutrition. Eating disorders can lead to physical problems such as brittle bones and anemia, and can also contribute to depression. It's important to note that people who have anorexia, for example, are fifty times more likely to die of suicide than the general population. Eating well and properly is not just about performance, it is also about your mental health.

After a meet or a workout session, replenish carbs, minerals, and water. You may need to replenish during a meet or workout if it is especially long. Aim to have a snack or drink every fifteen to twenty minutes. Sports bars and drinks are popular among athletes, but fruit and fruit juices are also good choices. One of the best foods for recovery after an event is milk. It provides a balance of protein and carbohydrates, and has calcium, which is especially important for female athletes.

DOPING

Doping, or the use of performance-enhancing drugs, is prohibited in track and field as it is in all athletics. However, banned substances are still used by some athletes and their trainers. An athlete who has been found to be doping may receive a competitive ban, but enough bans can prompt a ban from the sport entirely. The World Anti-Doping Agency (WADA) is responsible for determining which substances are banned in athletics, but newer drugs are always being developed that allow athletes to pass doping tests while still competing unfairly.

Not just Olympic and professional athletes experiment with performance enhancing drugs. An increasing number of young athletes are also seduced by the promise of an extra performance edge. Two of the most common drugs are anabolic steroids and creatine.

Anabolic steroids are an artificial version of testosterone, the male hormone. Female athletes have used them to gain muscle mass and lose fat in an unhealthy way. Steroid use saw a strong uptick starting in the 1970s.

MARION JONES

One of the most controversial and shocking lifetime bans was given to Marion Jones, an American athlete who won three gold medals at the 2000 Summer Olympics in Sydney, Australia. Jones excelled as a track and field athlete early on, winning the CIF

California State Meet in the 100-meter sprint four years in a row, but even in her high school track career, there were accusations of doping, and Jones had to go to court. She won the suit. Later, she was selected as the Gatorade Player of the Year for track and field for three years in a row. She then went to the University of North Carolina on a scholarship for basketball, and helped her team win the NCAA championship in her freshman year. At the Olympics in Sydney, after Jones' three gold-medal wins, her husband, who was an admitted steroid user, said that he saw her inject steroids into her stomach in the Olympic Village. Jones denied the claims, but eventually confessed in 2007 when she was stripped of her titles and banned from track and field.

Marion Jones is pictured at a track and field event at the Sydney, Australia, Olympics in 2000. She was later stripped of all her gold medals.

One popular chemical used among athletes is called creatine. It is a chemical normally found in the body, mostly in muscles, and can be obtained from certain foods. However, it has been synthesized to be used as a drug. Creatine has been shown to increase athletic performance, particularly in sprinters, but there has been little testing to draw conclusions about its effectiveness and its side effects. However, there is concern that it has negative effects on the kidney, liver, and heart, and that in combination with another herbal supplement, it can cause stroke.

Performance-enhancing drugs such as steroids are now banned from sports, but some athletes still use them during training and in competition. Doping scandals have been the downfall of many athletes include Dominique Blake, a sprinter from Jamaica was was given a temporary ban in 2006 and a longer ban in 2012. Yelena Churakova, a Russian hurdler, was banned for two years starting in 2013. Lada Chernoval, a Russian javelin thrower was issued a lifetime ban for doping in 2013. She had a previous temporary ban in 2008. Unfortunately, doping continues to be a practice used by many athletes with the WADA investigating athletes all over the world.

If you feel that your diet is lacking an important element, then talk to your doctor or a nutritionist. It's better to get your competitive edge from food rather than drugs.

CHAPTER FOUR

TRACK AND FIELD EVENTS

Thanks to Title IX, schools and universities have ample opportunities for female athletes to participate and train properly for track and field events. Track and field is both an individual and a team sport. Individuals participate in each event but come to the meet (and train) as members of a team. Athletes are scored on their individual performances but sometimes are also awarded points that are tallied for a team score. There are several organizations that govern the rules of track and field. The IAAF is one of these that oversees international rules, but each country has their own governing body, such as USA Track & Field. World-class meets such as the Olympics, Paralympics, and world championships pit competitors on a world stage, but they are not the only international meets. The South American Championships in Athletics, the European Athletics Championships, the Asian Athletics Championships, and

A team from Berkeley, California, shows off its medals during a meet.

the African Championships in Athletics are also international competitions that pit athletes in a particular part of the world.

World meets such as the Olympics only keep individual scores (but everyone likes to keep a medal count for their country). National meets among colleges and universities are team scored. How many points an individual performance receives varies from meet to meet. Meets can take place at indoor or outdoor tracks, permitting a longer competition season. The indoor track season usually lasts from January through March and most schools and colleges have track seasons that last throughout the school year.

Running events can be held year-round. Cross-country (long distance) events are usually held in the fall in the United States, while the international community holds them in the winter. The United States and Canada move track and field indoors during the winter. Sometimes this causes events to be eliminated or modified because of space considerations.

WOMEN'S SPORTS SINCE TITLE IX

Although Title IX attempted to bring much-needed equity to the field of sports, forty years after it was passed into law, women's sports still remain behind men's in dollars spent, television airtime, and even available opportunities at colleges and universities. The women who have benefitted from Title IX are also disproportionately suburban, wealthy, and white. A report from *Mother Jones* states "75 percent of white girls play sports, compared to less than two-thirds of African-American and Hispanic girls, and about half of Asian girls." The disparities continue at the collegiate level with African-American women best represented in basketball and track and field, and Latina women making up just four percent of total college athletes.

School and club meets are generally one-day events. Larger championship events often need at least two days. Many field events have qualifying rounds. At smaller meets, participants have three tries at each event with the top six to nine finishers moving onto the next round. Larger meets add an additional round to accommodate the larger number of participants.

Competition is a healthy aspect of sports, as well as of life, as long as you keep it in perspective. This means realizing that it is not all under your control. You might have an off day; many athletes do. It's important to keep your focus on how you perform rather than on the outcome of a competition.

Teams train together so that they can work well together on the playing field. However, that does not mean you will always be in sync with your team members.

Get enough rest on the night before a meet. Also, taper off your training right before the event. That means cutting back to have enough energy left for the meet.

PLAYING AS A TEAM

Teams of athletes travel together to the same meets to compete against other teams, but they also sometimes compete against each other as well. Teammates should be there to support each other regardless of who wins, but sometimes emotions run high and people's feelings can get hurt, or you might be worried about hurting someone on your team. It's okay to beat your teammate at an event. When you get out on the track or step into the launching circle, you can only focus on your own performance. Sometimes, unfortunately, your teammate might be angry. Let her know that you were only doing your best, not focusing on beating her. Clear communication and understanding help build a better team. If tensions run high, talk to your coach or team manager about resolving the conflict. It's

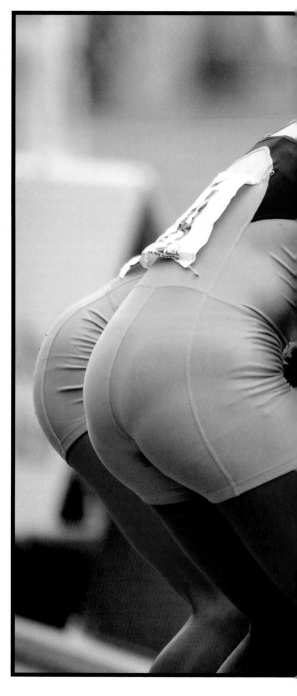

Looking out for your team members as well as other competitors shows that you are a good sport. No medal should be as important as the health and well-being of a fellow athlete.

important to have a team that works together so that you can perform even better as a unit.

BEING A GOOD SPORT

Being a good sport is not just about playing by the rules. It is also a code of conduct governing how athletes and spectators show

Lolo Jones clears a hurdle during a 100m heat in Sacramento, California. Jones is one of the sport's best athletes.

good discipline, respect, and self-control. Sports are more than just the final outcome. The enjoyment of the game is part of the experience, and it is difficult to enjoy track and field if everyone isn't being a good sport.

Some good rules to follow are to start by respecting yourself, which means staying away from performance-enhancing drugs, training properly, and being familiar with the rules of the meet and the location. Athletes should also be respectful of their teammates and their opponents and always play fairly by following the rules and the rulings of the governing officials. It's nice to offer encouragement and support to teammates, but there is no rule against offering it to competitors as well. But most importantly, being a good sport means showing grace in the face of defeat as well as in victory.

THE FUTURE FOR WOMEN'S TRACK AND FIELD

Women in sports are gaining more and more recognition, and many spectators show up for the championship track and field meets that are held each year. Girls don't have to see their athletic careers end after college or the Olympics, and they don't have to choose between sports and academics, either. Sports scholarships are offered at schools across the country, from Ivy League schools to state universities.

Many athletes become coaches for schools and universities. Others become personal trainers who focus on one or two athletes. There are many options available to you.

You don't have to be a professional athlete to continue competing as an adult. There are plenty of recreational clubs for adults.

Just because they aren't "elite" doesn't mean a lack of competition or commitment to the sport, so you don't have to worry about losing your edge. A love of the game developed now can last well into your adult life.

The benefits of fitness and the love of competition can help you in all areas of your life. A strong and healthy mind and body is something you can develop through participation in track and field. There is an event for every kind of athlete. Go out there and find yours.

TIMELINE

776 BCE The start of the ancient Olympic games, held in Olympia every four years. No women were allowed at the games, not even as spectators.

490 BCE Pheidippides carried the news of the Persian landing at Marathon to Sparta, beginning the tradition of running a marathon of 149 miles, the distance from Marathon to Sparta.

1851 Amelia Bloomer recommends women were pants that would bear her name, enabling wome to participate in a wider range of activities.

1860s Track and field athletics arrives in the United States.

1896 The first modern Olympic Games are staged with track and field as one of its major events.

1900 Women compete in the Paris Olympics.

1912 The IAAF (International Amateur Athletics Federation) is formed. It is track and field's first governing body.

1921 Representatives from six countries form an athletic federation for women. They merged with the IAAF in 1936.

1920s Women's track and field events in China are criticized.

1922 The AAU (The Amateur Athletic Union) opens track and field events to female athletes.

1928 Women's track and field becomes a part of the Olympic Games with five events. Kinue Hitomi wins a medal for Japan at the Olympics. Her win improves respect for women athletes in East Asia.

1932 Babe Didrikson wins the team championship at the AAU national track and field meet.

1948 Alice Coachman wins a gold medal in the high jump at the Olympic games, becoming the first African-American woman to win an Olympic gold medal. Starting blocks and wind gauges are introduced to the games. They allow for faster sprints and more accurate field statistics.

1960 Wilma Rudolph becomes the first woman to win three Olympic gold medals in track and field at a single Olympic Game.

1966 Roberta Gibb runs and finishes the Boston Marathon. She is the first woman to do so, but she was not officially entered in the race.

1968 Wyomia Tyus wins two consecutive Olympic gold medals in the 100-meter dash. Dick Fosbury introduces a new way to do the high jump called the Fosbury flop. It becomes the standard technique for the high jump.

1972 Congress passes Title IX of the Education Amendments of 1972. Women are finally allowed to run in the Boston marathon.

1980s Several world records are broken and many track and field athletes become household names including Zola Budd, a middle-distance and long-distance runner who broke the world record in the women's 5000-meter and was a two-time winner at the World Cross Country Championships in 1985 and 1986. Florence Griffith-Joyner was another top athlete in track and field in the 1980s, and she is still considered the fastest woman of all time because of world records that she set in 1988 in the 100-meter and 200-meter dash that remain unchallenged.

1982 The IAAF drops amateurism from its requirements for membership. It is now called the International Association of Athletics Federation. Athletes now can receive monetary compensation.

1987 Jackie Joyner-Kersee is the first female athlete pictured on the cover of *Sports Illustrated* magazine.

2000 Pole vault for women debuts at the Sydney, Australia Olympics.

2007 Marion Jones pleads guilty to charges of using performance-enhancing drugs. She retires from track and field that year.

2010 Amy Palmiero-Winters, a marathon runner and triathlete who lost a foot in a motorcycle accident, uses a prosthetic to continue to compete in marathons. She is the overall winner of the "Run to the Future" twenty-four -hour race in Glendale, Arizona, completing 130.4 miles. She becomes the first amputee to qualify for the U.S. National Track & Field Team.

2012 For the first time in Olympic history, female athletes from the U.S. outnumber male U.S. athletes. More women earn medals for the U.S., China, and Russia than the men.

GLOSSARY

AGILITY The ability to move quickly and easily.

ANOREXIA An eating disorder that involves compulsive dieting and extreme thinness.

ANTI-INFLAMMATORY A medicine used to reduce or control swelling.

BATON A hollow cylinder passed from one member of a relay team to another.

BICEP A large flexor muscle found on the front of the upper arm.

BULIMIA Compulsive overeating followed by self-induced vomiting.

CARBOHYDRATES A substance found in foods such as rice, bread, and potatoes, which provides heat and energy to the body.

CARDIOVASCULAR Related to the heart or the blood vessels.

CENTRIFUGAL FORCE A force described in physics that causes an object moving in a circular path to push out and away from the center.

COMPRESSION The act of pressing or squeezing something, such as an injury site, to reduce swelling.

DISQUALIFIED Prevented from being a part of something by an official or governing body because of an error on the part of the person or team.

DOPING The use of performance-enhancing drugs, especially in athletics.

HAMSTRING A muscle at the back of the upper leg.

HEPTATHALON A track and field competition comprised of seven events.

LIGAMENT The band of tissue that connects bones and holds organs together.

OSTEOPOROSIS Bone density loss resulting in brittle bones.

PACE The speed that allows you to perform your best as you run a course.

SYNTHESIZED Something made by combining other things through a chemical process.

TENDON The tissue that connects muscle to bone.

TRICEP A large muscle at the back of the upper arm.

FOR MORE INFORMATION

Athletics Canada

2445 Saint Laurent Boulevard, Suite 606

Ottawa, Ontario K1G 6C3

Canada

(613) 260-5580

athcan@athletics.ca

http://www.athletics.ca

The goals of Athletics Canada include increasing membership in athletics programs, supporting athletes in the Olympic and Paralympic Games as well as World Championships, and providing positive experiences for all athletes.

LIVESTRONG.com

1655 26th Street

Santa Monica, CA 90404

support@livestrong.com

http://www.livestrong.com

The LIVESTRONG community is dedicated to the promorion of a healthy lifestyle through fitness and healthful eating. They believe that healthy living prevents cancer and other dis-eases. LIVESTRONG is committed to helping people through education.

National Track League

2445 St. Laurent Boulevard, Suite B1-110

Ottawa, ON K1G 6C3

Canada

(613) 260-5580

http://www.nationaltrackleague.ca

A part of Athletics Canada, the National Track League keeps
records of all track and field events, records made, and
prizes won and live streams competitions.

Road Runners Club of America

1501 Lee Highway, Suite 140

Arlington, VA 22209

(703) 525-3890

office@rrca.org

http://www.rrca.org

The RRCA is the oldest and largest national association of
running clubs. It is dedicated to promoting running as a
competitive sport and a healthy exercise. The club supports
all runners regardless of ability or age.

USA Track and Field (USATF)

132 East Washington Street, Suite 800

Indianapolis, IN 46204

(317) 261-0500

dhtrack@aol.com

http://usatf.org

USATF is the volunteer-run national governing body for track
and field in the United States. Its mission is to drive competitive excellence in the field and encourage participation
and engagement.

USA Track & Field Foundation

c/o D.T. Moore & Company

217 North Lincoln Avenue

Salem, OH 44460

(412) 398-2484

http://wsatffoundation.org

The purpose of the foundation is to attract funds to develop
track and field programs for youth and emerging athletes.
The foundation also helps Olympic hopefuls and aids Team
USA through a grant program along with other financial
support.

U.S. Track & Field and Cross Country Coaches Association

1100 Poydras Street, Suite 1750

New Orleans, LA 70163

(504) 599-8900

www.ustfccca.org

This nonprofit organization represents cross country and track
and field coaches at all levels, representing over eight thou-
sand members in the United States.

WEBSITES

Because of the changing nature of Internet links, Rosen
Publishing has developed an online list of websites related to
the subject of this book. This site is updated regularly. Please
use this link to access this list:

http://www.rosenlinks.com/IX/Track

FOR FURTHER READING

Blumenthal, Karen. *Let Me Play: The Story of Title IX: The Law That Changed the Future of Girls in America*. New York, NY: Atheneum, 2005.

Bryant, Jill. *Women Athletes Who Changed the World*. New York, NY: Rosen Publishing, 2012.

Fitzgerald, Matt. *Racing Weight Cookbook: Lean, Light Recipes for Athletes*. Boulder, CO: Velo Press, 2014.

Gergen, Joe. *The First Lady of Olympic Track: the Life and Times of Betty Robenson*. Evanston, IL: Northwestern University Press, 2014.

Housewright, Ed. *Winning Track and Field for Girls*. New York, NY: Checkmark Books, 2009.

Jones, Marion. *On the Right Track: From Olympic Downfall to Finding Forgiveness and the Strength to Overcome and Succeed*. New York, NY: Howard Books, 2011.

Lang, Heather. *Queen of the Track: Alice Coachman, Olympic High-Jump Champion*. Honesdale, PA: Boyds Mills Press, 2012.

Magill, Pete. *Build Your Running Body: A Total-Body Fitness Plan for All Distance Runners, from Milers to Ultramarathoners—Run Farther, Faster, and Injury-Free*. New York, NY: The Experiment, 2014.

Malaspina, Ann. *Touch the Sky: Alice Coachman, Olympic High Jumper*. Park Ridge, IL: Albert Whitman & Company, 2011.

Mills, Gordon. *Born to Run*. New York, NY: Nelson Thornes Ltd, 2014.

Rappaport, Ken, *Women Athletes Who Made a Difference*.
    Atlanta, GA: Peachtree Publishers, 2010.
Smith, Maureen Margaret. *Wilma Rudolph: A Biography*.
    Westport, CT: Greenwood Biographies, 2006.
Stout, Glenn. *Yes, She Can! Women's Sports Pioneers*. New
    York, NY: Houghton Mifflin Harcourt, 2011.
Taggart, Lisa. *Women Who Win: Female Athletes on Being the
    Best*. Emeryville, CA: Seal Press, 2007.
Wade, Mary Dodson. *Amazing Olympic Athlete Wilma Rudolph*.
    New York, NY: Enslow, 2013.

INDEX

ABOUT THE AUTHOR

Myrna Carroll is a former track and field athlete. Her best events were the shot put and javelin throw.

Claudia B. Manley is an author who lives in New York with her son, partner, and cat.

CREDITS